RATIOS AND RATIONALE

DECODING THE PERCEPTIONS OF A SOUTH ASIAN NUCLEAR TRIANGLE

VAIBHAV SUNDER

Made with ♥ on the Notion Press Platform
www.notionpress.com

To our security forces

Contents

Contents

Foreword

"Terrorism has no nationality or religion." -- Vladimir Putin

"We want deeper sincerity of motive, a greater courage in speech and

earnestness in action".

- Sarojni Naidu

"While normal Hindus have India's interests at heart, the abnormal ones lay store on the Muslim interests in India!"

— B.S. Murthy

"Call it India or Bharat, but not Hindustan. Because no matter the intellectual stupidity of linguistic origin, in practice calling India Hindustan is like still calling humankind mankind."

— Abhijit Naskar, Making Britain Civilized: How to Gain Readmission to The Human Race

"If any young soldiers of today should read the book, they may understand that while the face of war may alter, some things have not changed since Joshua stood before Jericho and Xenophone marched to the sea"

-G. MacDonald Fraser, Quartered Safe Out Here! - A Recollection of the War in Burma, 1995

Preface

The aim of this text is to show why a nuclear triangle in South East Asia must be sinked. That by use of force or creation of strength all three countries - Pakistan, India and China have much more to lose. Because they are all developing nations, which large carbon footprints and a deep poverty index to manage. Why they should spend so much on nuclear and defense purposes is questioned and then a desire expressed to re-route such finances to development is the core thesis. We, as Indians must be unveiled to the Permanent War or Jihad of Pakistan, despite them being blood brothers till just a few decades ago. Chinese are one of the few non-Abrahamic countries and basing our foundation on that, both markets must work together instead of against to the benefit of West Asian and Westphalian countries.

The book is sprinkled with quotes from the authority on war studies Colin S. Gray

Acknowledgements

I am always thankful to my family and friends who help me in my endeavours

Prologue

Pakistan seeks to create credibility with nuclear weapons. China seeks to enforce its future dominance of the markets by show of power by nuclear weapons. India's narrative is purely defense from the start. And all three countries would do better by diverting such funding to economic development instead of getting pats from various countries around the world for who they are and what they all three represent - a mass of people who have to work hard to uplift their respective people from striking human rights abuses, poverty and building national identities based on economic progress and secular principles. The narrative for Indians is mired by untransparent questions as a defense. When Chinese troops crossed into the LAC in Ladakh the H.H. Dalai Lama's birthday was around the corner. When they crossed into Tawang a few years later, there was His Holinesses anniversary of the Nobel prize. When Pakistani militancy revived in Kashmir, Indians believe it is for the remaining Kashmir. The truth is, it is indoctrinated belief that Hindus are to be converted by force and even reasoning to Islam. It is a Forever War or Jihad as has been outlined in several books. The third, currently mild front is Tamil and Sri Lanka based African pressures. They have although disbanded for now. An intellectual pursuit for progress continues there. With a sarcastic tone, one may say they are less violent. However Easter bombings in Sri Lanka and the recent terrorist attack in Puducherry show the influx of Northern ideologies is acidicly seeping down to the South.

CHAPTER ONE

Symbolic Matters & Manipulation by Necessity

What the ex-Prime Minister of Pakistan Imran Khan and Bilawal Bhutto Zardari agree on, is that India is like the Nazi Germans and that nuclear use policy is on the table. This is extremely dangerous terriroty. It may result in leaders of all three countries, mired by an epidemic, with personal losses and domestic resentments push for unity agreements by harming each other. What the Pakistanis and Chinese and Indians agree to is that Westphalia has to end and stop at that, instead of calling Hindus and Indians Nazis, who defaced our religion by using European Monadistic Hinduism. And killing Jews, where Israel recently has excavated a Tel which is of Indic heritage as early as December 2022.

"In Italy, for thirty years under the Bourgias they had warfare, terror, murder, bloodshed - but they produced Michelangelo, Leonardo Da Vinci and the Rennaisance, In Switzerland they had brotherly love, 500 years of democracy and peace, and what did they produce? The cuckoo clock"

- Harry Lime, in the movie The Third Man, 1949

If the above quote were true today, the Koreans should be much more efficient than just producing Samsung and K-Pop. And the Japanese would not be creating plastic and neon environments and dreaming in Autumnal tempers.

CHAPTER TWO

Peaceful Dissent in Times of Covid-19

"As in any field that straddles science, policy and politics, the temptation to overreach is considerable. High demand for unwaffled answers create a market for study products that package immature theories as final easily digestible truth"
Bruce G. Blair, The Logic of Accidental Nuclear War, 1993

Pakistan shot it's protesting ex-PM a few months ago, he survived. Europeans have rioted on losing football matches to Islamic countries. India saw riots and killings of people who supported a politician who defamed the Islamic Prophet (S.A.W.S).

Now, in China when the Pinks protested lockdowns, they were opened and a new wave hit the country. This not only speaks of inequaility but even global pressure mounting on the intellect of the Asian systems.

CHAPTER THREE

The Russian-NATO conflict

"There is no hierarchy among the elements of war - one cannot pretend that one is more important than another" - J.Colin, The Transformation of War trans. LHR Pope Hennessy, 1912

Europe has an energy crises, food crises and yet it refuses to listen to quell war. It is astounding that Russian way of warfare throughout history is being ignored and that the sheer force it slowly exerts upon winters as witnessed by Napoleon Bonaparte, Adolf Hitler is being forgotten.

CHAPTER FOUR

After the Cold War, came West Asian conflicts

"The Clausewitzian world which has endured for three thousand years of recorded history, will also hold sway in the next century. It is not that the entire weight of the past says so, everything we know about the nonlinear, incalculable world indicates that we will not ever achieve predictability given natural phenomena"
Williamson Murray, The 1996 RMA Essay Contest, Joint Force Quarterly, 1997

"The war is over. Now the real fight begins" - Afghan Proverb

Not only this affirms that the Asian outlook of the Other is not Monadical but that the Occident simply cannot accept the Oriental philosophy despite severe and brutal bloodshed for decades. In fact, all their taxpayer money is getting wasted in Africa because they are unable to bring progress. And sadly, even China is making incorrect moves in Africa.

CHAPTER FIVE

Narratives to War, Questioning the Conduct of Peace

"An understanding of war requires its contextualization. Military history exists in a context of other histories" - Jeremy Black, 2004

Bilawal Bhutto Zardari went to the extent of saying, while in America that Russian fuel to India isn't even discounted, in smiles. China, has repeatedly encroached on LAC and is building infrastructure, thereby forcing the Indian government to route expenditure away from development into doing the same. That when a simple meeting between the two sides can quell billions from going into defense infrastructure and into civil and development infrastructure and capacity.

CHAPTER SIX

Manipulated by External Historical Necessity - History, Religions and Indians

Indian history despite being such a pluralistic society is one of dominating narratives, that are even hegemonical.

Like most historically colonized Asian countries. Hegemony is guided by manipulation intended with the necessity of the aggressor to aggrandize. The history in question is indeed of human beings, but it is written in letters and words where the spirit guides the word of the legal-historical world who has changed it over time. In school some of us were taught that India has never invaded another country for millenniaand yet quietly the textbooks of the British people today writes of Hindu kings who indeed did the sacrilege. When Taimur turned towards India, there was a failed check by Persians. When the British came here the Dutch were not congnizant of the historical problem being created.

Then, although Buddha, a revisionist to the present Orthodox systems, rebelled and tried to seek reverse spirituality, one from the heart by way of intelligence, his brethren over time, were angered. Intelligence always generates immense anger and energy, and thus monks and their supporters burnt down cities when questioned by the traditional clergy in the history books of India.

Chinese kings burnt all their libraries and wrote the I Ching on tortoise shells.

That is the only starting point today. Buddha is the first proselytiser and onwards came three successive hegemons in Abrahamic areas today. The Eastern world wrapped its ideals and principles in Buddhism and were cut into for centuries.

Because the Indian community created their folds, they were exempted from pressures and not just because they were Asians. Gradually human history was embalmed and embargoed, each successive war bringing more pious stretch outs towards the unseen realm to defend the word to each.

CHAPTER SEVEN

Forever War - The Doctrines of Harb and Jihad, Three pronged challenges to the Sovereignty of Indian Nation

Therefore, today Charles Sobhraj will kill those who do not understand Russian. Kashmir even if given away will not stop the metal hordes to seek a conversation of bad people. Africa wonders why Sri Lanka and Tamils hold sway in times of European and West Asian sway. And the Chinese decided the epitome of philosophy is material and accepted the Favela gangster Karl Marx and have created a brute machine where their anger to the world's deprivation is not towards the eastern front but towards those who house their small migrant population that thinks it is better to unite the world and speak of peace then only brute smoke chugging materiality. Tibetans. Repeated militancy by Pakistan since traditional wars failed, have created a game of dividing the Indian people. When a strike is made by lone suicide strike, the ground workers even in India are pressured to choose a better leader for the block level representation in elections. At lesst a new impression is made. The militants come from Pakistan and the rest of the West Asian world. There is pressure also from Southern LTTE legacy in Sri Lanka and Tamils. The Tibetans are manipulated by Chinese aggression.

CHAPTER EIGHT

False Narratives - Economics and Political Weakly

The narrative in the popular world is completely different. Truism creates the biggest revolutions, for then it is debated. And thus, Kashmir is a land of Muslims and they want to be India but for insurgents from Pakistan sponsorship.

China comes to Indian Ladakh when their migrant monks want to celebrate birthdays or have an anniversary of the Nobel peace prize. And the rest of the world, sells India weapons in clubhouse fashions when neither of the three nuclear armed countries - India, Pakistan and China are meeting the demands of the people who are the bottom of the socio-economic ladder. India by claiming democracy and deep religious bent. For all religions. Despite being called heretics by the Conservative and Radical thinkers in West Asia and Europe. Pakistan is thus the most liberal flavour of Islam. China by claiming that it is Communist and works for the man on ground level. They have very little groundwater left.

CHAPTER NINE

The black triangle and economics - Rise of the Other

In reality, China has no groundwater. Their biggest angst is with Japan and Europe and nothing really with India other than one of ideology, to which India seeks to accommodate always to prevent a backlash in the backyard. This is the political history of independent India. Pakistan cannot find a way to relay enough for the Forever War and yet develop it's own people off and away from the streets. Europe and the Americas now face the word with a reply after decades from Russia. Africa has been colonised and cannot find a way out of debt and doctrinations from the Semetic world. India has a shaken market and faces aggression in multi-pronged administrative problems after it's isolation in Asia where everybody else will agree to Chinese alternativism if not Chinese Communism.

And thus militancy in a three pronged war engulfs India every decade since a few decades after independence. China does it by galloping border areas on high altitudes, Pakistan by a steady stream of militancy on India's Western borders and Northern borders. Drugs, money and arms getting dropped by drones every other moment. Kashmir is split and yet Turkey is exerting over Indian cyberspace. There is a Arab university coming up in PoK. Tamils are currently forming one of the most Left governments under M.K. Stalin in the countries history. Sri Lanka is dead broke.

An Indian student in America presented a paper on Sanskrit on interpreting Sanskrit for a doctorate which said that when there are two rules to interpreting a text in Sanskrit. Use the one of the right. Right in Hindi is read as Dahina. It comes from Dakshin. Which means southern. Which means even the South when Leftist in present polity is going it wrong.

"Error in strategy can only be corrected in the next war" - Anonymous

CHAPTER TEN

The Questionable Nature of Heathen Laws, and Why They Bug the World - Defining Indian Territorial and Identity Manifestation Problems.

Indian laws define a democracy, a judiciary and a legislature. Americans have the highest incarceration rates right now, and yet people in India are reading the laws and battling American and European criticism. Prince Faisal Al-Turki, a retired intelligence royalty from Saudi Arabia admits as recently as this year, that since the departure of non-reasoning-based jurisprudence, that is the first millennium, they face injustice and hardships across all the lands they live and speak in.

Orthodox countries are again in stand to vote for economic power since the Soviets disbanded. Now, China has a big problem of hard material progress to divide in a populace when they are aided by a system of politics that has long been criticiced for, not only it's misgivings but also failure in non-Orthodox countries. Such as the Latin American continent, that faces extremely high numbers in organised crime.

In such a present, India is in a deadlock. Not only do we have American alliance that historically always nests and will mean permanent problems with China, if not more. Russians will be forced to side with China, when they are a closer political and military system to our history. Kinder leaders of Pakistan cannot help us, when they themselves are troubled by a need to assimilate the rest of the Western Asian problems

"When the goodman mends his armour,
And trims his helmet plume;
When the goodwife's shuttle merrily,
Goes flashing through the loom
With weeping and with laughter
Still is the story told
How well Horatius kept the bridge
In the brave days of old"
-Thomas Babbignton, Lord Macaulay, 1842

CHAPTER ELEVEN

Blind men feel a sinking ship - questioning perception

If the Chinese continue on a straight material path, they will end up the next America. The problem is not that they will do so, but the way in which they are doing it. Debting all it's neighbours, Africa and at a later point creating a final East-West divide.

When seeking solutions, one is shown of the Tibetan-Mongoloid interlocking realities as a system in Sacred Mandates: Asian International Relations since Chinggis Khan by Timothy Brook, Michael van Walt van Praag, Miek Boltjes.

The question is not whether they will win as a thought form of ideology, but then simply a seeking to accelerate their progress. Irrespective of ideology. Then the Pakistan-Chinese formation can be finely looked into and an Indian identity created

Imam Sadiq (A.S.) of the Persian Twelvers said this out directly that do not expect an apology from the Left and an error from the Right.

Therein hangs the mess that can be scaled by near-old Theological progression. Therein dies the hallmark of modern political thought, in a truism that does not change and will bleed us all. Therein is a superior Persian Identity to understand of the Jurisprudence of Imam Sadiq (A.S.). And apply to statecraft and policy-making for peace.

CHAPTER TWELVE

The World of Warfare - Cheating Emptiness and Tragedy in Material People into Mass Movement Assent

The thinking knows the force emptiness and existentialism poses to the world of 2022. In developing countries it is very easy to substitute this with Nationalism, Socialism and even religion. These deep ended feelings are exactly what the Russian crises with NATO brings post-Covid. Leaders across the world are successful when they fuel this pain in people. All doctrinations in Islam and dare I say Chinese is borne of this emptiness.

The Europeans wrote of it in Sartre, Camus and others. However, when we see the country for what it actually is, or the society or even the religions a wholly different fervor fills us. One that is Orthodox. One that takes patience, time and money.

"Patriotism is the last refuge of the scoundrel." - Samuel Johnson

CHAPTER THIRTEEN

Pulsating into a moderate guideline

No amount of statecraft can create any total and complete equality. Not money, not religion and not even enforced laws. And violence is our resort at the smallest impunity. It is not to policy then, that we must turn but a belief that mass movements avert the truth. Truth averts the world at large. The world is then again, actually still medieval to begin with temporally, only we call it the dark ages in all world histories except Africa. Which is still waiting to write and eat and is the dark.

"There is no "modern" world. As future crises arrive in steep waves our leaders will realize that the world is not "modern" or "postmodern" but only a continuation of the ancient - a world that, despite its technologies, the best Chinese, Greek and Roman philosophers, would have understood , and known how to navigate" - Robert D. Kaplan, 2002

"The pace of progress in AI is incredibly fast. Unless you have direct exposure to groups like DeepMind, you have no idea how fast -it is growing at a pace close to exponential. The risk of something dangerous happening is in the five-year time frame. 10 years at most." - Elon Musk commenting on Edge.org

Mainstream Further Reading And Institutions

Fighting to the End: The Pakistan Army's Way of War, C. Christine Fair, 2014

In Their Own Words: Understanding Lashkar-e-Tayyaba, C. Christine Fair, 2018

The Hundred-Year Marathon: China's Secret Strategy to Replace America as the Global Superpower - Michael Pillsbury, 2019

Some active institutions on the matters -

Force magazine India

Observer Research Foundation

Asia Society

Manohar Parrikar's Institute for Defense Studies and Analyses

Centre for Policy Research

Manekshaw papers

Oryx

Centre for Land Warfare Studies

Delhi Policy Group

Research paper - Neo-deterministic seismic hazard scenarios for India - A preventive tool for disaster mitigation. (Journal of Seismology) by Imtiyaz A. Parvez, G.F. Panza and 8 others.

www.ingramcontent.com/pod-product-compliance
Lightning Source LLC
La Vergne TN
LVHW041302150826
845673LV00008B/2698

* 9 7 9 8 8 8 9 2 3 4 9 4 4 *